ROTHERHAM PUBLIC LIBRARIES

The truth about
Guy Fawkes?

This book is dedicated to Julie Bell
and the librarians at Lancaster with thanks.

First published in 1996 by Franklin Watts
96 Leonard Street, London EC2A 4RH

Franklin Watts Australia
14 Mars Road
Lane Cove
NSW 2006

© Terry Deary 1996

The right of Terry Deary to be identified
as Author of the Work has been asserted
by him in accordance with the Copyright,
Designs and Patents Act, 1988.

Series editor: Paula Borton
Designer: Sally Boothroyd

A CIP catalogue record for this book
is available from the British Library.

ISBN 0 749 62211 3
Dewey Classification 941.06

Printed in Great Britain

The truth about Guy Fawkes?

A History Mystery

by

Terry Deary

Illustrations by Linda Birch

FRANKLIN WATTS

LONDON · NEW YORK · SYDNEY

Contents

Introduction

History is full of mysteries. Stories are passed down through the years and most of us believe them simply because they are written in books. But sometimes the writers get it wrong! History writers have been known to:

- make mistakes
- exaggerate
- invent 'facts'
- leave out important facts
- tell whopping great lies

This makes your job of understanding the past very tricky.

What is the truth? Who is telling it?

When a detective sets out to discover the truth he may have to solve a mystery. He must ask questions and work out who is lying and who is telling the truth. In this book that's just what you have to do. Become a history detective.

You will be given some fascinating facts mixed with some fascinating lies. Sort them out and solve the mystery. This *History Mystery* is arranged in three parts:

Part One

To make the mystery more enjoyable to read, it has been re-told in the form of a story. Imagine yourself in the shoes of two young detectives. Travel back in time to discover how they uncover the evidence.

Part Two

To help you understand the world in which the mystery is set, there is then a selection of facts about the people of those days and their lives. Some of these facts will help you solve the mystery, others are simply fascinating facts on their own.

Part Three

Finally the story ends with the characters reaching their own 'solution' to the problem. You might not agree with their solution – some historians would certainly disagree! But remember . . . it is *a* solution, not *the* solution. In history there is hardly ever such a thing as *the one* right answer. That's why history is so strange and irritating and enjoyable and infuriating. History is a mystery . . . and *that's* a fact!

Part One

The story of Guy Fawkes

1

4 November 1605 (morning)

The empty eyes of the skulls stared down on us. They were perched on the towers that led on to London Bridge.

"Who are they, father?" I asked as I guided my horse towards the bridge.

"Traitors, son. Traitors."

I felt the lead-rope in my hand tighten. The girl had stopped her horse to stare up at the skulls. Her face was pale and frightened. We'd been travelling down from Lancaster for two weeks and I'd never seen her so scared. "Will they do that to *my* head?" she whispered and lifted her bound hands to her throat. A foul-smelling breeze from the Thames lifted her dark hair and she looked more like a wild-eyed witch than ever. She tossed back her hair – a sure sign that she was a witch, my father had told me.

My father gave a harsh laugh. "No, girl," he laughed harshly. "They'll just hang you and throw your body in a ditch. Try and magic your way out of that, witch-child," he sneered.

She looked at him with all the hatred I knew she felt. I wanted to say, "Sorry, Ellie," but my father would have beaten me if I'd shown any weakness towards the convicted witch-girl.

"Come on, John," my father ordered and led the way

over the bridge. London Bridge is one of the wonders of the world, he'd told me. It certainly was a wonder. The bridge was lined with tall houses that jutted out over the river. Crowds jostled us as we passed on the narrow roadway, merchants pushed forward to sell you food and drink, beggars whinged their pleas for money, men stood in secret huddles and spying eyes watched our every step.

The shadows of the houses closed over our heads. Our home town of Lancaster had nothing like this – apart from the heads on the castle walls. Here there were so many people. I didn't know there were so many in the world.

And there'd been no other city on our journey to compare with London. My father led his horse carefully through the masses and I followed, leading the girl. People stepped out of the way of her horse when they saw she was a prisoner. A girl like that could only be guilty of one crime: witchcraft.

And the courts *had* found her guilty back in Lancaster. Along with five other women she'd been sentenced to hang for her crime. My father had been building the scaffold for them when a messenger arrived from London. I'd been cleaning out the castle stables and my father marched in.

"We're going to London," he'd said shortly.

"Why?" I asked. I'd never been further than the coast a few miles away. London was a world I'd only heard about.

"King James has this interest in witchcraft. He wants to talk to one of the witches," he explained.

"Which?" I asked.

"That's what I said, stupid boy," he snarled.

"I mean, which one of the witches?" I asked.

He shrugged his wide shoulders. "Any one. But the old women wouldn't last the journey and some of the younger ones are dangerous. We'll take the girl," he decided. "Pick the three best horses, pack some saddlebags with food. We leave tomorrow." He turned on his heel and left.

So, we were taking the girl. I'd seen her when I served food to the prisoners in the Well Tower dungeon. Some wept, some screamed, one sat in the corner of the cell and mumbled to herself. But the girl just sat. Her large, dark eyes followed me round the cell. She never spoke. The only expression on her face was contempt. I was an assistant jailer, I would lead her out to her execution one day soon. She hated me.

I discovered her name was Ellie. Her crime was that her grandmother had been accused of witchcraft, so all the family were accused, too. Ellie had also cared for a neighbour's cat when the old woman was out. The court had decided the cat was the old woman's 'familiar' – the Devil in animal form – and Ellie was guilty of caring for it.

In court she had simply said it was a cat. "I fed it and loved it. It never spoke to me. It isn't a devil and I'm not a witch." They didn't believe her and sentenced her to die with the others.

I'd watched a few people die at Lancaster Castle. Catholic priests who died for their religion and even a man accused of witchcraft. None had been as young as her. It had bothered me. My father simply enjoyed it all the more. "All the wickedness in the world is little compared to the wickedness of a woman," he said.

"Is it?" I asked.

"It says so in the Bible." He took me by the shoulders and shook me. "If you want to save your soul then keep away from women. Especially witch-women like the ones in the castle. The world will be a cleaner place when we've hanged this lot," he said.

The castle executioner always wore a hood so no one would recognise him. Everyone knew it was my father. I respected him. Feared him and loathed him – but respected him. He was my father. If he said women were evil then I believed him. I never asked him about my mother. She'd died giving birth to me. I never dared ask him if she'd been evil too.

The journey to London passed mostly in silence. My father spoke only to give me orders. When we stopped at wayside taverns he spent the night in the alehouse while I was left to guard the girl. A stable with some filthy straw was usually good enough for her bed, but it was still cleaner than the Well Tower dungeon.

Ellie rarely spoke. October storms shook the stable one night. I asked, "Are you frightened?" but she just stared at me with a half-smile then turned to look at the glittering rivers of lightning in the sky. I began to wonder if she had caused the storm. On All-Hallows' Eve, when witch-power was at its greatest, I asked her if she would fly away.

"Fetch me a broomstick," she said. I found one in the stableyard. "Now untie my hands." I fumbled with the rope till it fell off her wrists.

She climbed the hayloft till she reached an open window high up in the gable end. A cold wind lifted her hair and a colder moon glinted in her eyes.

She looked down to where I stood, far below. "I am not a witch," she said. She swayed on the sill and leaned forward. "Shall I jump? I will if you ask me."

"No!" I cried, suddenly afraid. But I was afraid that she would kill herself and my father would blame me for losing a prisoner. I was ashamed of my cowardice. "No – please," I said.

She climbed down and held out her wrists for the rope. "Never call me witch again," she said before she burrowed back into the straw in the corner.

"I won't," I promised.

Now, on London Bridge, I'd seen her afraid of the grinning skulls. Afraid for the first time.

2

4 November 1605, afternoon
They said that Ellie was evil. But I never saw true evil till I
saw the Tower of London that day. Out of the mists of the
Thames rose its grim grey walls. The smell of the pigs kept
under their shelter was sickening. And, over everything,
hung an overwhelming feeling of death.

Cruel-beaked ravens stared down from its walls and
somewhere within the walls some strange creature roared
like a devil in torment. The guard at the gatehouse checked
my father's documents and sent for the governor. We
waited in silence, watching the bustling workmen dragging
cartloads of stone and mortar to build new walls.

Carpenters were hewing and planing at planks of wood. No
one looked happy.

The governor walked slowly, stiffly towards us. A tired
old man with small eyes that looked sharply down a long
nose. A ruff at his neck pushed his square beard upwards
and gave him a bristling fierceness. "I'm William Waad,
Lieutenant-Governor of the Tower."

"Sergeant Edward Kendal, Lancaster Castle," my father
said. He didn't introduce me or the girl.

Waad's thick moustache turned up in an imitation of a
smile. "Lancaster. Good. A fine castle," he said.

"Not so fine as the Tower of London," my father

replied, clearly trying to make a good impression.

Waad began to walk towards the great tower in the centre and my father fell into step with him. "Don't you believe it, Kendal. When I took over from Sir George Hervey two months ago the place was a shambles. Doors left open everywhere. No control over who visited prisoners, who came or who went. I've increased the guards, I'm having new walls built . . . and more doors closed. People come here to *suffer* a little, Kendal."

My father nodded in eager agreement. He knew all about making people suffer. "No one's escaped from Lancaster in the twenty years that I've been sergeant there," he said grimly.

Waad stopped and looked at my father carefully. "I have trouble finding enough good men, Kendal," he said. "Honest and trustworthy men. There are dangerous tasks ahead of us and I'd like your help in a little adventure we have planned for tonight."

My father's back stiffened still more, till it was straight and rigid as his sword. "Yes, sir."

Waad put an arm around his shoulders and began to lead him up a flight of stairs. He seemed to remember Ellie and me at last. He turned. "You, boy, see to the horses. The girl can work for her keep while she's here." He turned to Ellie, "Find the kitchens and they'll give you a job . . . maybe they'll let you feed the cats," he said with a grim chuckle. "Witches *like* cats, don't they?"

"I'm not a witch," Ellie replied boldly.

Waad looked down his long nose. "You were tried and found guilty. After you've talked to the king you will hang."

"I'm innocent," Ellie said.

The old governor shrugged and looked over the green lawn with a wooden block in its centre. "So were half of the heads that have rolled off that block in the last hundred years. If it suits the state to have you dead then you shall die. What's *innocence* got to do with it?" He turned away without waiting for an answer.

Ellie helped me find the stables and settle the tired horses in their new home. She was good with animals. She seemed to know their ways and talked to them in no language I'd ever heard. Is it any wonder she frightened me?

Then we found the kitchen. A huge, stone-floored, steaming room full of squabbling, hurrying, greasy-clothed men, women, boys and girls. Ellie walked up to the man who was giving the most orders. "I've been sent to work here by Mr Waad," she said. "He said I could feed the cats."

The fat cook grinned a black-toothed grin and pointed to a tub of stinking meat on the floor beneath the table. "Give them that," he smiled. "Hope you're a fast mover."

"What do you mean?" I asked.

The man's bloodstained hand pointed at me. "The last keeper of the cats tried to play tug-of-war with the mother cat. She won the meat then took his arm as well. Heh! What a mess!"

I shivered and wondered what sort of cats these were. When I'd helped Ellie carry the tub of rotten meat to the menagerie I found out. They were huge, tawny beasts with golden eyes. "Lions," a toothless old woman explained as

we looked over the wall into the pit where they stalked angrily. "King James is fond of lions. They're on the flag of Scotland, you know."

I nodded dumbly. Ellie began to throw the meat into the pit and the beasts tore into it growling. "Save some for the cubs," the woman said.

She led us to a small, stone-walled garden. Two clumsy cubs with huge paws were rolling on the grass and sparring with each other. They looked up when Ellie opened their gate. "Don't go in!" the old woman warned. "Even at that age they'll tear your skin to shreds!"

Ellie ignored her. She walked to the centre of the grass, mumbling softly. The creatures circled her. Suddenly they sat down quietly. Ellie reached out a hand and began to stroke one behind the ear. The other rolled on its back and allowed her to stroke its belly. "Never seen anything like it," the old woman mumbled. "Is she a witch?"

"Yes," I said before I could stop myself.

3

5 November 1605, midnight
Our sleeping room was a windowless hut leaning against the wall of the Tower. We were expected to find our own blankets and space in the flea-infested straw. I was tired and fell asleep wondering how long I'd have to stay here. I wanted to be back in my room at Lancaster Castle with the fresh smell of the sea on a good day.

I hadn't seen my father since Waad took him away on some duty. When the night was at its darkest and quietest he shook me awake. "Up, boy," he ordered.

He held a smoking torch that spluttered in the foggy night air. I shivered and yawned. "What? Are we going home?"

He grabbed me roughly by the shoulder and pulled me out of the hut. A dozen armed men stamped their feet to keep warm. Torches flared and sparkled on their armour. My father spoke in a low, rough voice, "I've work to do for the governor."

"At this time of night?"

My father slapped my ear with the back of his leather-gloved hand. "Don't ask questions. Just listen. The king wants to see the witch-girl . . ."

I opened my mouth to ask, "What – now?" but remembered myself in time. "Yes, father."

"Montague here will row you to Whitehall Palace," he explained, nodding towards a skinny, sour-faced man of about thirty years. "You will escort her. If she tries to escape you must kill her."

"Yes, father," I said.

"If she succeeds in escaping then kill *yourself*," he hissed. "If you don't then I will," he promised.

He turned on his heel and joined the band of armoured men. Montague pulled on a rope and dragged Ellie from the shadow of a doorway. We followed the men to a gate that led on to the black swell of the Thames. At first I thought they were going with us. My father's troop climbed into a low barge with six oars and I saw Waad helped to a place in the stern. We scrambled into a tiny skiff and the dumb Montague rowed it out into the blackness.

The freezing mist cut us off from the rest of the world in minutes. Then, moments later, the soldiers' barge disappeared and we were alone in the silent night, black as a Tower raven's wing.

Ellie's eyes caught a faint glimmer from the lantern. She seemed to be looking through the fog. "There's something happening out there. Something important." I have never had witch powers. But that midnight in London I too could feel something.

We heard, but couldn't see, the water splashing on the piers of London Bridge as we passed under it. Then there was silence until we reached the quay beside Whitehall Palace. Speechlessly, Montague tied up the boat and led the way to a door at the side of the palace.

Men on horses clattered in the torch-lit courtyard. So much movement in the dead of night. Ellie was right about this being an important night. Montague led us to a side door, muttered a password to a sharp-eyed guard and led us into an entrance hall. Another word to a serving man and we were led up dark stairways and along endless oak-panelled passageways.

Montague stopped at a door, knocked and pressed an ear against the thick wood to hear a reply. He opened the door and nodded for us to enter.

The man in the small room was a beetle. Hunched, round-backed and black-gowned. His dark eyes were the most intelligent I had ever seen. Dark eyes set in a pale, sickly face over a neat, pointed beard. The eyes summed us up in seconds. "The witch?" he said.

"I'm not a witch," Ellie said tiredly.

"I am the Earl of Salisbury," the beetle-backed man said softly. "I am the king's chief minister. Tonight is a busy night. An important one. We are expecting visitors later in the night. You will keep the king entertained and awake while he awaits the news. You understand?"

"Yes, sir," I said. Ellie stayed sullenly silent. The Earl of Salisbury stepped closer to her. "It would be wise of you to be respectful to his majesty, my child. He is a powerful man. He has the power of life . . . and death. If you amuse him then he may feel generous towards you," the old man explained. "He is fascinated by witchcraft. He's written a book about it," the earl said. "Just answer his questions politely," he advised. He turned to me. "You, young man, will act as guard. If the girl makes any move to threaten the king, then kill her."

That was the second time tonight someone had given me that order. "I know," I mumbled, fingering the dagger at my belt.

The beetle-backed man raised a yellow claw of a hand and said, "But otherwise keep that knife well out of sight. His majesty has a curious fear of the cold steel of weapons."

"Yes, sir," I said.

The intelligent eyes crinkled into a sudden and unexpected smile. "Good luck," he said.

He led the way to the door, opened it and announced, "The witch-girl from Lancaster, sire. Elizabeth Grey."

A glowing fire lit and warmed the room. After the dank November air of the Thames the warmth wrapped itself around me. Tapestries covered the walls to keep out the draughts. There was even a carpet on the floor.

I'd expected to see a man with a crown sitting on a throne. But King James was seated in a comfortable chair with a warm woollen robe wrapped around him. A flask of wine stood on the table by his side and he kept filling a crystal goblet and drinking deeply from it.

His limpid eyes were like those creatures that the fishermen brought to Lancaster Castle and his straggling beard was sparse as winter grass. As he drank, his over-large tongue seemed to push the wine on to that beard and he mopped at it with a silken handkerchief. He wore gloves.

"Stand here, girl," he said.

His Scots accent and blubbery lips made it hard to understand what he was saying at first. Ellie hesitated and the Earl of Salisbury pushed her forward before he crossed to stand behind the king's chair.

"You know you're a sinner?" the king said.

"I'm not a witch," Ellie said quietly.

"When we are born we are fated to go to heaven or hell when we die. You will go to hell, child."

"Where will you go?" Ellie asked.

The chief secretary's bright eyes widened with alarm.

"It is not done for a subject to question a king," he said sharply.

King James waved a limp hand. "But I will answer her," he said. "In the Bible, Proverbs chapter 8, verse 15 says, '*Through me kings reign.*' Even God calls me a god," he explained. "But, when I take my throne in heaven, I can put in a word with God for you if you confess freely to me. On judgement day he may raise you up. Why are you condemned?"

"My grandmother . . ." Ellie began uncertainly. "Gran . . . begged a crust from a miller. He threw her out on to the road and left her to starve. She cursed him and his family. Within a month his daughter died. He said the curse came from the devil. He accused her of witchcraft."

"The law in England is just," the king pronounced. "She'd have had a fair trial."

"She was left to rot in Lancaster Castle until she confessed," Ellie told him. I felt sickened. I knew I was one of the jailers who let the prisoners suffer with the worst food in the dampest of stinking cells.

"There would be other witnesses," the king said.

"There *were* people who said they had suffered from Gran's witchcraft too. They also named my mother and my sister . . . and me," she went on.

The king sighed. "In Scotland we burn witches. At least you will die mercifully on the end of a rope in England," he said.

Ellie gave a small choking cry and began to move forward. I caught her arm and dragged her back but didn't touch my dagger.

Just then there was a soft knock on the door. The Earl of Salisbury hurried to open it. An armed man stood there. His black beard was cut square and his eyes were hard as the executioner's axe.

It was my father.

4

5 November 1605, 4 a.m.

He stepped to one side and allowed Lieutenant-Governor William Waad to come into the room followed by a man with chained wrists.

Waad bowed low but a little stiffly. "I apologise for this disturbance, your majesty, but we have uncovered a plot. A plot to explode a large quantity of gunpowder under the Parliament building. It would have killed everyone, including your majesty, at the opening of Parliament, if we had not uncovered it," Waad went on.

I tugged Ellie backwards and into the shadow of the door.

I glanced at the king. He had a curious stare on his cold-fish eyes – excitement but no fear. If he wasn't afraid of a plot to blow him to his heavenly throne then he was braver than the Earl of Salisbury said . . . or he was prepared for this sort of news. The king nodded. "A powder plot, eh, Waad?"

"Yes, sire."

"You know how I hate the thought. My own father died when his house was blown up, did you know that, Salisbury?"

The chief minister nodded his head, "Indeed, sire."

The king rose to his feet and walked slowly round the

prisoner. The man was tall, well-dressed and with red-brown hair and beard. His smock looked like a servant's but his fine boots and spurs were those of a gentleman. "What is your name?" King James asked.

"John Johnson," the man replied calmly. He had a gentle northern accent.

"And no doubt you are a Catholic, my friend."

Johnson seemed to think of this for a moment. "I was born a Protestant," he admitted, "but was converted to the Catholic faith as a youth."

James nodded. "No doubt you think I am too harsh in my laws against the Catholics?" the king asked.

"Unjust," the plotter said carefully.

"And who do you think would make a better monarch?" James asked.

Johnson shrugged. "Perhaps your cousin, Lady Arabella Stuart."

"She's a Protestant too," James said.

"With a weakness for the Catholic religion," Johnson said quickly.

"Is that so?" the chief minister put in. "Perhaps we ought to investigate this dangerous lady a little more closely," he suggested to his master.

James nodded lazily. "Once we have found out who put Mr Johnson up to this powder plot, eh, Salisbury?"

"Indeed, sire," the little minister bowed.

James stood and faced the prisoner. "Well, Mr Johnson? Who paid you to commit this *treason*?" He said the last word carefully. Everyone in the room knew that the punishment for murder was hanging, but the punishment for treason was the much slower and more agonising death of hanging, drawing on the rack and being cut into quarters.

"No one *ordered* me," Johnson said.

James nodded again. "So, you are saying you planned

this treason alone?"

"Yes."

"You laid up stores of powder under Parliament alone?"

"Yes."

"And no one else knew about it?"

"No one."

"Then who knew enough to warn Lord Monteagle?" James leered. I jumped at the name. Lord Monteagle's estates were in Lancashire and he often visited Lancaster Castle. "Last week our Catholic friend Lord Monteagle received a letter. You have it, Salisbury?" the king asked his chief minister.

"Your highness," the minister said and took a piece of paper from a table. He held it up to a candle.

"Read it, Salisbury," King James commanded.

The minister began, "*My Lord Monteagle, for the love I bear to some of your friends I wish to preserve your life. I would advise you to come up with some excuse to avoid attending the opening of Parliament, for God and man has come up with a way to punish the wickedness of these times. Retire to the country where you will hear news of the event in safety. Though there will be no appearance of any trouble I tell you this Parliament will receive a terrible blow, yet they shall not see who hurts them.*"

The earl stopped and looked up. "Someone knew enough of the plot to warn Lord Monteagle not to go to Parliament. Did you write this letter, Johnson?"

The prisoner seemed to have lost his confidence now. He simply shook his head.

"Someone betrayed you," King James said. "Tell us who was behind this plot and we will find them and punish them."

For a long time the only sound in the room was the soft crackle of coal and logs on the fire. Finally Johnson said, "No one."

James spread his hands helplessly. "If you won't tell us of your own free will, Mr Johnson, then we will have to let Sir William Waad and his little torture machines *persuade* you." The king nodded towards my father who seemed to be leading the guard. "Take him to the Tower and use all the means you have to get at the truth."

5

5 November 1605, dawn
I woke with a start on my straw, stiff, cold and tired after
my disturbed night. I trudged wearily to the kitchen for
some bread and cheese. Ellie was making herself useful and
seemed to have the job of taking breakfast to prisoners in
the Tower as well as to King James's lions.

' She returned from one journey to the cells and said,
"Your father's on guard on poor John Johnson's cell. He
wants to see you."

"*Poor* Johnson? He tried to murder the king!" I told
her.

She looked at me seriously. There were shadows of
tiredness under her eyes after our disturbed night but those
eyes were as bright and clever as the Earl of Salisbury's.
"Not everyone accused of a crime is guilty," she reminded
me.

"And you think Johnson's innocent?" I asked.

"I think he's a *good* man," she answered carefully.
"Whatever he was doing he believed it was for the best."

I shrugged and set off in search of my father through
the maze of corridors and twisting stairways. I was lost
three times before I finally found him. "Are we going home
now, father?" I asked.

"Home!" he barked and stuck his black, spade beard

out. "Certainly not. I've a job to do here. Sir William Waad wants me as a guard when the Powder Plot traitors are brought in . . . and I'll be needed as a witness."

"Witness to what?"

"To the arrest last night," he said.

"What happened, father?" I asked.

He sat down heavily on a stool at the door to the cell. He was tired too, though he would never admit it. "The king's officers went to inspect the cellar under Parliament at midnight last night, and caught Johnson there," he explained.

"Why did they go there?" I asked suddenly.

"Why? To check that the Parliament buildings were safe," he growled as if I had asked a stupid question.

"Sorry, father, I meant why midnight. It seems a strange time to be searching a cellar. Why not search it during the day?"

He rubbed his beard. "That was the time when they would be likely to catch the traitors," he shrugged.

"But how did they know the traitors would be there?" I persisted. "You were ready to leave the Tower before midnight. Sir William Waad must have known an arrest would happen before the officers captured Johnson."

"The traitors would come at night to check the gunpowder, wouldn't they?" he said.

"But how did the officers know there was gunpowder there?" I went on. "They must have known about the gunpowder first – remember the letter to Lord Monteagle? They found the gunpowder in the cellar and left it there."

"The barrels were hidden under piles of firewood and iron bars. We uncovered some of it last night," my father told me.

"The officers must have found it then covered it up again. Why? They could have made it safe as soon as they found it. But they didn't. The officers came back at midnight to catch the plotters in the act. It makes a better story, doesn't it?"

My father's face creased as he thought about it. "The officer in charge was holding John Johnson when we got there. We were just sent to escort him to the Tower. We could see that Johnson had been laying trails of powder – a sort of fuse, ready to light when the king reached Parliament. I thought at the time it was odd."

"Why, father?"

He looked at me with those hard eyes. "You've handled the cannon on the walls of Lancaster Castle, haven't you? You know enough about gunpowder to work it out for yourself. How do you look after gunpowder?"

"Keep it dry," I told him.

"Exactly. Lay a trail of gunpowder at midnight, put a match to it ten hours later – and what will happen?"

I saw what he meant. "Nothing! On a misty November night . . ."

"In a damp cellar by the river . . ."

"It would be useless within the hour!"

"Johnson must be a fool!" my father spat.

"He doesn't look so stupid," I said.

"Then the people who gave Johnson his orders were fools," my father sighed.

"Or very, very clever," I muttered. I thought about the cleverest man I'd ever met. It was a shock to see him standing there. The beetle-backed chief minister, Salisbury, was looking at me sharply. I wasn't sure how much he had heard. "Good morning, my young friend," he said.

I muttered a shy, "Good morning, sir."

Father jumped to his feet. "You wish to see the prisoner, sir?"

The earl nodded and my father opened the door. "Come in," the earl ordered. "This is a desperate man and he looks too strong for me. Bring the boy too."

My father and I went into the room and stood
nervously by the door while the chief minister sat on a stool
at the foot of the bed. Johnson sat on the edge of the bed
and looked at him boldly. It was the first view I'd had of
Johnson in the daylight. He must have been about thirty-
five years old. His clothes were of good quality but a little
worn, like a man who has done a lot of travelling.

"I hope you slept well, Mr Johnson," the earl said.

"Your accommodation is most comfortable," Johnson
answered coolly. "But your servants forgot to leave me a
key."

The minister gave a thin smile and said, "Perhaps you
are used to rougher beds, Mr Johnson. Perhaps you have
slept on the ground?"

The prisoner nodded. "You are right, sir. I have been a soldier."

"Fighting with the English regiment in Holland, I'd guess."

Johnson nodded graciously.

"In the service of our old enemy, the Spanish," the earl guessed. "Was it the Spanish who paid you to assassinate King James? Or was it the Pope himself?"

Johnson grinned widely. "I decided to do it myself, as I told the king last night."

The earl brought up his hunched back in a massive shrug. "It doesn't matter, Mr Johnson. You see, no matter what you say the people of England and Scotland will blame the Spanish, the Catholics and their Jesuit priests."

"The people of England know that James is weak and a slobbering dog, not fit to rule a kennel. You rule the country, my lord Salisbury," he said.

The chief minister gave a secret smile then went on, "And, thanks to you, the people of England will be horrified by this outrageous plot. They will hate the Catholics more than ever and will turn their grateful love to James . . . the English will remember your name – and the fifth of November – for hundreds of years. They will despise that name."

Johnson's mouth twitched with a small smile. Salisbury's keen eye noticed it. "By the way . . . what is your name?"

"John Johnson."

"No," the minister breathed. "Your real name. We found a letter in your pocket with another name on. You may as well tell us the truth."

The man looked through the narrow window to where the ravens fluttered like black funeral banners in the colourless sky. He turned back to the minister. "My name is Fawkes," he said. "Guy Fawkes."

6

10 November 1605
In the days after the arrest of Guy Fawkes, everything – and
everyone – changed. My father became accustomed to his
new role as a warder in the Tower. He began strutting
around and giving orders just as he had done back in
Lancaster Castle. And when I asked him about going home
he answered, "Why should we?"

My father made sure I was given a properly paid job as
a junior guard – hours of boring duty at doors and odd
spells of carrying messages for prisoners. On 7 November I
helped unload almost a ton of gunpowder from Guy
Fawkes's cellar into the Tower storeroom. I began to settle
into the old building and know its dark passageways even
without a lantern. But I didn't feel at home as I had back in
Lancaster.

The biggest change was in Ellie. She began to forget
the cruel deaths of her family and the shadow of the noose
around her own neck. She became one of the most popular
kitchen girls, and some time in the next week remembered
how to smile. Towards the end she even began smiling at
me. No one looked less like a witch, I thought.

As I guarded Guy Fawkes's cell one afternoon she
brought food for the prisoner and some extra for me. "I
made it myself," she said shyly. "Tom, the cook, lets me

cook things now."

"There's too much here," I told her. "Would . . . would you like to share it?"

She nodded and sat on a stool opposite me, her thin back pressed against the stone wall. "How is Mr Fawkes?" she asked.

"Weaker every day," I said. "Most days they take him to the dungeons under the White Tower and the earl or Sir William question him. I think he's told them very little."

"He's brave," she said. "But the government know everything about the plot . . . it's all we talk about in the kitchens! Guy Fawkes was the first one they caught, but it wasn't his plot."

"It was some Catholic gentleman, wasn't it?" I said. The guards didn't gossip the way the kitchen staff did but I'd picked up some pieces of the story.

Ellie leaned forward, chewing on her food and talking quickly. "It was a gentleman called Robert Catesby who started it all. He'd been fined and imprisoned for being a Romanist Catholic so he got two friends – Thomas Winter and John Wright – and told them he wanted to blow up Parliament. They didn't know enough about gunpowder so Thomas Winter went over to the Netherlands and found an old schoolfriend who was an expert."

"Guy Fawkes," I nodded.

"That's right. They rented a house next to the Parliament buildings and started to dig a tunnel through the walls and under the House of Lords. But they were gentlemen – they weren't used to that sort of work – and they had problems with damp from the river seeping in, so the tunnel was going really badly. They had to bring other people into the plot – some to dig and some to give money for the gunpowder. In the end there were thirteen plotters."

"But they must have got through in the end," I said.

"No! An amazing thing happened. One day they were

digging when they heard a roaring sound above them. It sounded like a river over their heads. They were terrified. They sent Guy Fawkes to see what it was and it was coal being piled in the cellar over their heads. That cellar was directly under the Parliament chamber . . . and it was for rent!"

"So . . ." I said slowly, "they rented the coal cellar?"

"That's right! They paid off the coal merchant and started loading gunpowder into the cellar. It was so easy – and so much drier, of course."

"My father said the powder barrels were covered with bundles of firewood," I said.

"I heard that. Anyone looking into the cellar would have just seen firewood. The opening of Parliament was put back to the fifth of November, so they had plenty of time to get it all in place. They say there was enough powder there to blow the building up three times over!"

"It's as well it was discovered when it was," I said.

Ellie leaned forward and looked at me seriously. "I don't think so, John," she said. "I don't think there was ever any chance of James being blown up. The Earl of Salisbury knew about the plot long before the fifth of November!"

I nodded. "There was that letter to the Romanist Catholic Lord Monteagle warning him not to go to Parliament," I remembered. "Someone betrayed Guy Fawkes," I said. "Who?"

Ellie stood up and brushed crumbs off her thin and shabby dress. "Why don't I ask him?" she said.

7

It was against every rule of the Tower. "No one's allowed in to see the prisoner!" I told her.

"Except a servant bringing him his food," she said.

"But I have to make sure you leave the tray and walk straight out," I said.

"Stand at the door," she said. "Tell me if anyone appears. I'll walk straight out. No one will know how long I've been in there."

"I can't," I moaned and saw myself stretched on the Tower rack. I could imagine the pain and could hear myself crying the way I'd heard other prisoners crying in my worst nightmares.

Ellie stood close to me. "John," she breathed. "Guy Fawkes is suffering because he is too brave. If I can explain that there's no need to protect his friends – tell him that the government knows everything – then he'll confess. It'll spare him any more torture. Do you want him to go back on the rack?" she asked.

That wasn't a fair question. "Of course not," I mumbled.

"Your father does," she said. "Your father loves making people suffer. Are you like him?"

"No!" I hissed and heard the word echoing off the ancient walls. I slipped the key into the lock and opened the door. Guy Fawkes was lying on the plain wooden bed. He had lost his cheerful arrogance. He trembled as he turned to look at us and his eyes were sunk in grey pools of bruised flesh.

Ellie placed a hand on my wrist and squeezed it. "Thanks, John," she said. She knelt beside the prisoner and began talking to him while I turned back to the door and looked down the silent corridor. It was half an hour before the far door rattled open and Sir William Waad came towards me, followed by the shuffling figure of the Earl of Salisbury. My father locked the door behind them and escorted them towards the cell.

"Ellie," I whispered. She looked round, stood up quickly and collected the empty tray from last night's meal. As she reached the door my father was about to enter. She collided with him and the plates clattered to the floor.

"Clumsy witch-child," he growled.

Sir William and the earl waited patiently while she scooped up the debris. My father stood stiffly in front of the Tower governor. "Sir, this witch's execution has been delayed long enough. Permission to execute her today, sir?"

"Of course," Sir William said impatiently.

Ellie froze in the act of rising from her knees.

My father turned to me and his eyes were glowing with pleasure. "A little job for you, John. About time you learned the ropes, as it were. Hah! You can hang her, son."

I felt suddenly sick and his leering face became blurred. From the corner of my eye I could see Ellie sink back to her knees. For a moment there was silence then the little black form of the chief minister stepped forward.

"The girl was convicted in London, was she?" he asked.

"No. Lancaster," Sir William replied.

"Then I'm afraid the law says she must be executed in Lancaster," the earl said softly. "After all, the people of that town want to see justice done. The boy can take her back tomorrow." He looked at me with those intelligent eyes. "Justice must be done, John. I know I can trust you to see that the girl gets what she . . . deserves."

He said the last word carefully and suddenly I knew what he meant. "I will, sir," I whispered. My father looked a little cheated but slapped me on the shoulder. "Good lad," he said. I think it was the first time in my life that he'd praised me. It would be the last.

The earl turned away and looked into the open door of the cell. The prisoner was sitting on the edge of his bed. I didn't know what Ellie had spoken about but the man looked calmer now. He was no longer shaking. "Good morning, gentlemen," he said.

"Are you willing to confess, Fawkes?" Sir William asked.

The man rose from the bed shakily. "Yes," he said. "I think I am."

The governor seemed to take a step back in surprise. "Ah! Oh . . . John. Go to my office and bring my secretary. Tell him to bring paper and ink. Guy Fawkes is going to confess!"

I ran through the corridors and spun down twisting stairways but those stairways were straight compared to my whirling brain. Ellie would get what she deserved – the earl had made me her judge and my father had made me her executioner.

But I couldn't believe Guy Fawkes would get justice. And I couldn't work out who had betrayed him.

Part Two

The Fact Files

1. THE PEOPLE FILE

Who can you believe? Here are some true facts about the main characters in the story. What sort of people are they? Can you trust what they did or said?

Guy Fawkes

Name: *John Johnson (or Jhon Jhonson)* – the name he used while involved in the plot
Guy, Guye – Christian name
Guido – the Spanish version of Guy that he used when fighting for the Spanish
Fawkes, Faukes, Fawks, Faux, Fauxse and Faulkes – various ways his surname has been spelled

Appearance: Strong, tall and powerful. He had reddish-brown hair and beard and probably grey-blue eyes.

Character: Brought up near York in a strict Protestant family until his father died when Guy was about nine. His mother remarried a Catholic and Guy converted. He joined the Spanish Catholic armies fighting in the Netherlands where he became an expert in using gunpowder. He had shown courage in battle and showed even more under torture. He was intensely loyal to the other plotters and suffered a lot of pain rather than betray them.

Problem: Did Guy Fawkes really expect the Gunpowder Plot to kill King James? Did he join the plot because he was a devout Catholic or because it was a well-paid 'job'? And, if it was a 'job', who employed him – the rebel Catholic lords, like Catesby, or King James and his cunning chief minister?

King James I

Name: *James I of England and VI of Scotland*

Appearance: Large ugly nose, small mean mouth, thin brown beard. His legs were weak and bowed so he walked clumsily and often rested a hand on someone's shoulder to steady himself. Spoke in a squeaky voice with a strong Scottish accent.

Character: Spent far more money than he could afford, drank too much and spent as much time as he could hunting. Because of his weak body he would often be tied to the saddle of the horse! Despite his bravery in the saddle he was terrified of knives and swords and always wore knife-proof jackets (worn till they were in tatters) to stop some assassin's dagger. His father had been murdered when his house was blown up and James feared that something similar might happen to him. He had some disgusting personal habits like spilling food from his mouth and picking his nose. He rarely washed his hands – just dabbled his fingertips in water at meal times; some historians believe he had a skin disease that made washing painful. He was very experienced at dealing with plots against the throne after thirty-five years of it in Scotland. Well-educated and, in spite of his feeble appearance, no fool. His mother, Mary, Queen of Scots, was executed by Elizabeth I – but ruthless James quickly forgave and forgot that in order to get Elizabeth's throne.

Problem: James was worried that the English would try to replace him with some other monarch or that the Romanist Catholics would rebel against him with the help of a Spanish force – as the Armada had tried to do to Elizabeth I in 1588. The threat of that Armada made the English rally round their queen and she became their heroine. Would a similar, terrible threat (like the blowing up of Parliament) make James equally popular? If James believed that then would he actually set up a plot to kill himself (knowing it would not succeed)?

The Earl of Salisbury

Name: *Robert Cecil*
Baron Cecil of Essendine
1603
Viscount Cranbourne 1604
Earl of Salisbury from
4 May 1605
The Pigmy – Elizabeth I's nickname for him
The Little Beagle Dog – James I's nickname for him
Parrot – James's other nickname, which the earl really hated.

Appearance: Robert probably had a fall when he was an infant and this may have caused the hump on his back. He also grew up very thin with spindly legs and was constantly ill. He was probably no more than 1.5 metres (5 foot) tall. At the time of the plot he had a greying beard, a high forehead and sad, thoughtful eyes.

Character: As a popular rhyme of the time said: *"Little Cecil trips up and down / He rules both court and crown."* That's not far from the truth. Elizabeth may have been his queen and James his king but it was Robert Cecil, Earl of Salisbury, who *really* ran the country. He was extremely intelligent and needed to be very cunning in a world full of plots and spies and assassins. If he was sometimes ruthlessly cruel it was because that was the only way to survive. He wanted James to be king because that was the best way to keep peace in the kingdom after Elizabeth's death. In fact he had been planning the takeover with James years before it happened – but he was careful never to mention the fact to Elizabeth! He knew that if James lost the throne he, Robert Cecil, would lose his life.

Problem: Would Salisbury make a plot against the king and blame it on the Romanist Catholics (as they were known at that time)? The Catholics were hoping that James would be kinder to them than Elizabeth had been. For a while James was but that began to change. Who were the secret Catholic enemies that James had to fear? How could Salisbury bring them out into the open? Invent a plot, invite suspected Catholics to join it . . . ? If they said "Yes" then he'd know they had treason at heart. The plot would give him an excuse to imprison or execute them. Would Salisbury be clever enough and able enough to manage this?

Robert Catesby

Name: *Robert Catesby*

Appearance: He wore red clothes whenever possible because he believed it suited his 'fiery' nature. He was tall, good-looking, athletic and a fine swordsman.

Character: When Catesby married he became a strong Catholic. On the death of his father in 1598 he inherited the family's estates, but Robert was wild and wasteful and always short of money. He took part in the Earl of Essex's rebellion against Elizabeth I in 1601. Essex was executed, but Elizabeth spared Catesby's life. His punishment was a huge £3,000 fine which forced him to sell his manor house. He sold more family property to raise money for another plot against Elizabeth – the woman who'd spared his life. When Elizabeth died he decided that James must die so Catholics could worship in their own way. He chose Parliament because that was where laws to crush the Catholics were made. "Maybe God designed that place for their punishment," he said. Catesby was also a liar. When Guy Fawkes was arrested Catesby rode to the Midlands to start a rebellion. "James has been blown up!" he told the rebels. A monstrous lie.

Problem: When Essex's rebellion failed, Catesby was fined but set free. Why? What did he promise in exchange for his life? Did he promise to set up a new, fake plot to see which traitors would join – then betray them to the Earl of Salisbury? Why else would he set up the Gunpowder Plot? The Catholics said it was because he was deeply religious, the Protestants said he was bloodthirsty. Or was he just a troublemaker who was wild enough to plot anything?

2. THE TIME FILE

1566 On 19 June Mary, Queen of Scots has a son, James Stuart. He is christened a Catholic. The Catholic religion is not popular in Scotland so . . .

1567 Mary, Queen of Scots is captured and forced to give up the throne to thirteen-month-old James. His father, Lord Darnley, has been blown up in a gunpowder plot – probably by his mother's new boyfriend! The child-king James is brought up as a Protestant.

1570 On 13 April a boy is born in York. He is christened Guy Fawkes in the local Protestant church.

1578 Guy Fawkes's father dies.

1587 Guy's mother marries Dionis Bainbrigge, a Catholic. Is this when Guy became a convert to the illegal religion? Meanwhile Elizabeth I has Mary, Queen of Scots executed. Mary's son, James, writes to Elizabeth to congratulate her! He is desperate for the English throne when the old queen dies. Guy Fawkes's mother and stepfather spend a lot of Guy's inheritance until . . .

1591 Guy Fawkes is twenty-one years old and now owns the estate his father left him. He promptly sells it. Was he short of money? Or did he simply want freedom?

1593 Guy joins the Spanish Catholic army fighting in the Netherlands. For adventure? For his Catholic faith? Or simply for the money? During the eleven years he is away . . .

1601 the Earl of Essex rebels against Elizabeth I in England, fails and is executed. Seven of Essex's supporters, including Robert Catesby, are spared. They will go on to create a plot to murder James I – the Gunpowder Plot. (James up in Scotland said he supported Essex's rebellion . . . until it failed!)

1603   Elizabeth I, the last of the Tudors, dies. She has no children and no close relatives. James VI of Scotland is the most popular choice as heir, so he comes south and becomes king of both countries. There are two plots that year to kill James – the Bye Plot and the Main Plot. They fail and the chief plotters are executed or imprisoned. This doesn't put off a new group of plotters led by Catesby . . .

1604   May: Thomas Percy rents a house next to the House of Lords and Guy Fawkes is brought back from the Netherlands to act as caretaker and to advise on explosives until on 11 December: The plotters begin to dig a tunnel from the house to the Parliament building but . . .

1605   7 February: The meeting of Parliament is postponed, so this gives the plotters more time. They struggle to break through the thick walls of the House of Lords. Then, in . . .

March they hear coal being loaded into a cellar above. This cellar is a perfect place for the Gunpowder Plot so . . .

25 March: They decide to rent this cellar and save all the digging. Powder is carried into the cellar. Parliament is now due to open on 5 November but . . .

26 October: Someone has sent a letter to the Catholic nobleman Lord Monteagle warning him to stay away from the meeting of Parliament on 5 November and avoid "a terrible blow". The plotters have been betrayed but they decide to go ahead anyway! So . . .

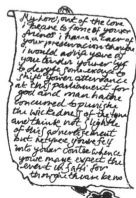

4 November: During a search of the cellar Guy Fawkes is discovered and arrested . . .

5 November: Fawkes is taken before the king but refuses to talk. When the plotters hear of Guy's arrest they flee to the Midlands, hoping to

start a rebellion anyway. The government already knows who these men are even though Guy Fawkes has refused to name them. But . . .

8 November: The plotters get no support for a rebellion. They are surrounded. Catesby and another plotter make a last stand, back to back – and are killed with a single bullet! Plotters who survive are arrested. When Guy is told this . . .

9 November: He finally confesses.

1606   27 January: The eight living plotters are taken to trial – it's all over in a day. They are found guilty.

30 January: Four plotters are hanged, drawn and quartered in St Paul's churchyard.

31 January: Guy Fawkes and the remaining plotters are hanged, drawn and quartered at Westminster. Their heads are displayed on spikes over London Bridge.

Remember, remember . . .

Since the Gunpowder Plot was discovered it has passed into English history.

Did you know . . .?

1. In January 1606 (before Guy Fawkes and the plotters had been tried and executed) Parliament passed a new law. It said that 5 November would become a holiday of public thanksgiving. People lit bonfires to celebrate and threw dummies on the fire dressed as Guy Fawkes. The first record of this is at Cliffe Hill in London where the Pope joined Guy Fawkes in the flames.

2. Sir William Waad, Lieutenant-Governor of the Tower, had a memorial made. It is a marble slab carved with the coats of arms of all the lords who judged the Gunpowder plotters. It is set in a wall in the Tower's council chamber. But there is an extra coat of arms on it – one that does not belong to a noble judge – Waad had added his own! After all, he had tortured the truth out of Guy Fawkes, hadn't he? He wanted to be remembered, too. But today it is the victim, Fawkes, who is remembered, not Waad, the torturer.

3. The government decided that the cellars beneath Parliament should be patrolled night and day to prevent another Powder Plot. That patrol was stopped a long time ago but a search of the cellars is still made before the opening of every Parliament.

4. At different times dummies of different people have been burned on 5 November. In 1850 a Catholic cardinal suggested that Britain should become Catholic again – his figure was burned. Seven years later the British people living in Kanpur in India were massacred by rebels led by Nana Sahib. So, on 5 November that year it was Nana Sahib's turn to sit on top of British bonfires.

5. In England there was a similar type of celebration on November 17 to commemorate the death of the last Catholic queen, Mary Tudor, in 1558. People went on celebrating this day for another 200 years.

6. Within a few years of the Gunpowder Plot people began to use fireworks on 5 November and still do to this day.

7. For many years the people of Scotton village in Yorkshire refused to celebrate 5 November with fireworks and bonfires. This village was where Guy Fawkes used to live and the people didn't think it was fair that Guy should take all the blame.

8. In Lewes, in Sussex, there is a 5 November tradition of setting fire to barrels of tar and rolling them down a hillside. This is extremely dangerous, of course, and the adults find it such hot, thirsty work they have to go to a local pub to drink and cool off. Or at least that's their excuse! As a little boy from Lewes wrote in 1822, *The fifth of November's a very good spree / Special constables all is as drunk as can be.*

3. THE LIFESTYLE FILE

The people of England and Scotland were horrified by the Gunpowder Plot. They thought the threat to kill so many people in one explosion was particularly shocking. Why? People were dying all the time, more slowly and more cruelly than in an explosion. Why were people not shocked by some of the other tragedies that happened in those days . . .

✗ In December 1596 seven people died of starvation on the streets of Newcastle. The following autumn twenty-five more died in just two months – but of course they were *poor* people so maybe they didn't matter so much?

✗ In 1603 hundreds of people died in London from an outbreak of plague – the coronation of James was postponed because of this – but that was natural and there was no wickedness involved.

✗ In London, in 1583, eight people died when a stand collapsed at a bear-baiting entertainment – but, of course, that served them right for enjoying themselves on a Sunday; this was God's will.

Would you have survived in the days of James I? Try this test to see how you would fit in . . .

True or False

1. If you were a gentleman you could keep pigeons in dovecotes in your garden. *The birds could be used to carry your messages. True/false?*

2. If you played village football then you would be part of a team of up to a thousand-a-side and the goals might be three miles apart. There were few rules, and riots or murders could happen during a game. *King James banned the playing of sports on a Sunday. True/false?*

3. James had a new Bible published in 1611. Before that you had to use the Geneva Bible. *This Bible was nicknamed the Breeches Bible because it said Adam and Eve "sewed fig leaves together and made themselves breeches". True/false?*

4. You would go to bed with a nightcap on because there were so many draughts. *However, doctors said there had to be holes in the top of the nightcap to stop the brain from overheating. True/false?*

5. You were advised to clean your teeth with powdered stone. *This removed the stains from your teeth. True/false?*

6. Teachers were highly respected in the time of King James. *True/false?*

7. King James believed that girls should be educated as well as boys. *True/false?*

8. Your breakfast would usually be a boiled egg and a glass of water. *True/false?*

9. If you were a boy you might be taught a business by a master craftsman. You would become his apprentice. *However, apprentices had to live by strict rules . . . including one that said you had to have your hair cut. True/false?*

10. If you saw a woman walking backwards it was a sure sign she was a witch. *True/false?*

Answers

1. *False.* Pigeons and doves were kept to be killed and eaten.

2. *False.* James wrote a book in which he encouraged people to play sports on a Sunday . . . after they had been to church.

3. *True.* For most families the Geneva Bible was the only book they ever owned.

4. *True.* But, while they wore nightcaps on their heads they didn't usually wear nightdresses or pyjamas.

5. *True.* Unfortunately it also removed the enamel from the teeth and allowed them to rot more quickly. So did the mouth-washes made with honey.

6. *False.* Many pupils admired their teachers, but the rest of the world didn't. Teachers were very badly paid (even though they worked from 7 a.m. till 5 p.m.) and had few holidays. Some had to take other jobs in order to make a living – William Swetman, for example, was also a fishmonger.

7. *False.* James was set against schools for girls. He said educating women was like taming foxes – the only effect is to make them more cunning.

8. *False.* Breakfast was usually a slice of bread, washed down with a drink of beer. River water was usually too unhealthy to drink. But even people who had really fresh water believed it was bad for your health.

9. *True.* Apprentices who grew their hair too long could be arrested, have a basin forced over their head and have the hair below the basin sliced off. They could also be sent to prison.

Girls could become apprentices to hatmakers and dressmakers but usually trained as servants.

10. *True.* That's what the superstitious people of James's time believed.

Crafty Crime

If you couldn't make an honest living then could you have made a dishonest one? Here are some tricks of the criminal's trade from the 1590s and 1600s. Become . . .

Whip jack

"I wonder if you could help me. I was a sailor in old Elizabeth's Armada and I helped to save England. Unfortunately, as we chased the Spaniards back to Spain we hit a storm and I was shipwrecked. I had to survive on an Atlantic island for ten years. Ten years of pay the navy owes me. If you could lend me a few pence I could make my way to London then I'll be a rich man. I pay you back ten-times over!"

Of course, you are not a shipwrecked sailor and if you are given money you will never see the giver again.

Abraham man

"Goodbye. What? Thank you. They say I'm mad. I'm not! Well, not very mad. Just a little. I thought I might sit on your doorstep for the next few weeks. I'll scare away those monsters I can see flying over your roof. What? Can't you see them? All I want is some food. No? Then you could always give me some money to go and buy some. I'd have to go away then and leave you in peace. Pity about those flying monsters. Hello?"

You may be given money to go away. But don't *stay* away! If they're daft enough to pay you once, they'll probably be daft enough to pay you again . . . and again!

Jarckman

"Good afternoon, sirs and madams. I am an official beggar. I have here a licence to beg, as you can see. It's not that I am too lazy to work. This licence confirms that I am in fact too sick to beg. Would you care to read it? You will see that the magistrate who signed it is from a town a hundred miles from here, but I can assure you that it is official. People like you, with money, really ought to give to official beggars like me."

A licence to beg is very hard to get. However, if you know someone who can write, then you can make a forged licence, can't you? Just make sure that the local constable can't check up on the magistrate who was supposed to have signed it.

Bawdy basket

"Good afternoon, my dear. I have some delightful trinkets here. Would you care to look? Lovely lace to decorate your dress or how about this real silk girdle — the colour goes perfectly with your eyes. Expensive? No! In fact I won't charge you a penny! You're obviously an important servant in this house. Just get me a nice piece of beef or mutton from your kitchen – maybe a couple of loaves of bread and some cheese. Your master will never miss food from all the stuff he has in the larder."

Just make sure the lace and silk are as cheap as you can get them – and make sure the servants get you food or drink that is worth ten times as much!

Frater

Good morning, madam. It's a lovely day, isn't it? The sort of day when you are glad to be alive and well. Of course, it's a pity when not everyone can be well. There are some very sick people in this town. The Council have appointed me to collect from kind and generous citizens like yourself. We are planning to build a hospital for the sick and the aged. If you could spare a few groats then you can be sure it will go to a really good cause.

The truth is that *you* are that 'really good cause' and all money collected will go straight into your pocket.

These tricks may seem silly to you. You may say you would never be caught out by people like this. But the truth is millions of people *were* tricked into giving money to fraters and jarckmen and all their crooked friends. And, amazingly, they still are today. In June 1995 a man and his wife were sentenced to jail for collecting thousands of pounds for a 'charity' that never existed.

Their trouble was that they were caught. In James's day it didn't do to be caught out in a crime or you'd suffer a . . .

Painful Punishment

Until 1597, six years before James came to the English throne, punishments had been terrible for 'vagabonds' – men and women who were homeless and who begged for a living. Between 1570 and 1575, in Middlesex, forty-four tramps were branded with 'V' for vagrant on their chests. Eight who did not learn from this lesson were hanged.

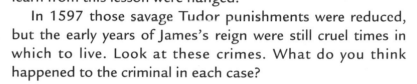

In 1597 those savage Tudor punishments were reduced, but the early years of James's reign were still cruel times in which to live. Look at these crimes. What do you think happened to the criminal in each case?

1. Thomas Pounde was a Catholic. He had been a friend of the great Catholic martyr, St Edmund Campion, who was

tortured and hanged by Elizabeth I in 1581. As a result, by the time James came to the throne, Pounde was an old man who had spent twenty-five years in jail. He objected to the cruelty of the law and the execution of the Bye Plotters. But what was his sentence?
a) A fine of £1,000
  b) The rest of his life in prison
  c) One ear cut off in London and the other cut off in Lancaster.

2. Farm workers were badly paid. They would often earn just £9 a year. A beggar could earn sixpence a day which was double the money of a farm worker. The townspeople were worried that beggars were also thieves so they were very nervous about strangers who appeared in town with no job, people we might call tramps. What did they do to tramps?

a) Put them in the poorhouse and made them work.

b) Gave them a meal and some money so long as they promised to move to another town.

c) Placed them in the stocks and whipped them.

3. Young apprentices were forced to wear plain clothes. To stop them sneaking home to change into something fancy the law said they must keep all their clothes under their master's roof, where he could keep an eye on them. One apprentice disobeyed. What happened to him?

a) He was hanged

b) He was stripped in front of the other apprentices and whipped

c) He was forced to cut up his fine clothes.

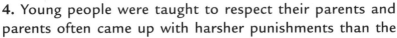

4. Young people were taught to respect their parents and parents often came up with harsher punishments than the

law! Peter Carew was bullied at school by one of the teachers. When he arrived home what did Peter's father do?

a) Tied the boy to his horse and led him back to the school

b) Caned the boy twice as hard as the teacher had, to show him how much better it was to be bullied by a teacher

c) Took the dog out of its kennel and chained Peter in its place.

Answers

1. a, b and c! The ear cutting was later changed. He had to stand with his head through a pillory and have his ears nailed to the wood on each side. However, they were not cut off.

2. c. A *local* beggar might be placed in a poorhouse and forced to work to pay for his/her food. But a strange beggar who wandered into town was often whipped or put in the stocks so he/she would not come back in a hurry.

3. b. Apprentices were not allowed to sing or dance in the streets either.

4. c. Peter was so distressed by the bullying teacher he had climbed to the top of the city walls and threatened to throw himself off if the master came after him. Peter survived the school . . . and his father's treatment.

Terrible Tortures

William Waad was made governor of the Tower of London eleven weeks before Guy Fawkes was imprisoned there. Waad was an expert at torturing prisoners, so having a man like him at the Tower was lucky for the Earl of Salisbury . . . unless, of course, the Earl of Salisbury *knew* about the Gunpowder Plot months before it happened. In which case the Earl of Salisbury may have given Waad the job with torturing the plotters in mind.

Eight years before the Gunpowder Plot a Catholic priest called Gerard had been captured by Elizabeth I's officers and brought to Waad for torturing in a different prison. Gerard lived to tell the story of his torture. If Guy Fawkes had lived he would probably have described the same thing . . .

"Then we went to the place of torture. We went in a sort of solemn procession, attendants going ahead with lighted candles because the place was underground and very dark, especially around the entrance. It was a place of enormous size and in it were all sorts of racks and other instruments of torture. Some of these they displayed to me and told me I should have to taste every one of them. Then again they asked me if I was willing to answer their questions. 'It is not in my power,' I answered. Throwing myself on my knees I said a prayer or two.

"They led me to a great pillar of wood that was one of the supports of this vast crypt. At the top were staples and here they placed my wrists in manacles of iron. They ordered me to mount two or three steps. My arms being fixed above my head they withdrew those steps one by one so that I hung by my hands and arms. The tips of my toes, however, still touched the ground since I was too tall. Since they could not raise me higher they dug away the ground underneath me.

"Thus hanging by the wrists they asked me if I was willing to confess. I replied, 'I neither can nor will.' But so terrible the pain that I was scarce able to speak. The worst pain was in my breast and belly, my arms and hands. It seemed to me that all the blood in my body had rushed up to my arms and hands. I was under the impression at the time that the blood actually burst forth from my fingers and at the backs of my hands, but this was a mistake."

Gerard hung there for an hour or so after the questioners left. When they saw that he was not going to talk they did a very clever thing. They left him with a jailer who treated him kindly. He wiped the sweat off Gerard's face and pleaded for him to confess because it was causing him (the jailer) so much misery! When kindness didn't work they tried horror – three or four men gathered in the chamber and talked aloud: "He'll be crippled all his life . . . if he lives through it. But, he'll have to be tortured daily until he confesses."

Gerard fainted after an hour, was revived with water and hung up again until he fainted again. This happened about seven or eight times that afternoon. Waad came back and asked Gerard to confess. Again he refused. Waad stormed off saying, "Hang there till you rot!"

Bravely, Gerard resisted three days of this treatment before he used a rope to escape from the Tower.

Guy Fawkes was just as brave and held out for several days. But Waad wasn't going to lose a second prisoner down a rope. Guards made sure there would be no escape for Guy Fawkes.

Fun and Games

People of James I's reign enjoyed all the cruel sports that they had had in Elizabeth I's reign: cock-fighting, bear-baiting, bull-baiting and so on. They also enjoyed the theatre. William Shakespeare was writing some of his best plays during the days of King James.

Nowadays Shakespeare's plays can seem rather old-fashioned. But when he wrote them they were bang up to date. Soon after the Gunpowder Plot William Shakespeare wrote a play in which a Scottish lord was involved in a witchcraft plot to kill the king and take his throne. James must have been delighted by Shakespeare's play, *Macbeth*.

Here's a five-minute version of the two-hour play. You might like to try it!

Macbeth
by William Shakespeare
& A. N. Other

Cast:

Narrator: Fills in the missing bits without being boring

Macbeth: Important Scottish lord, brave fighter on the outside but a bit scared of the dark

Lady Macbeth: Married to Macbeth. Not a happy woman. Wants to be queen by foul means or fair . . . preferably foul.

Witches 1, 2 and 3: Hideous creatures, men or women, young or old, but pure evil – good parts for teachers

Banquo: Macbeth's best mate. Brave, honest . . . and utterly stupid if he can't see what Macbeth is up to

Murderer: Not the sort you would trust to help old ladies across the road. No prizes for guessing what he does.

Macduff: Handy with a sword, loving husband and father. Unfortunately he's in the wrong place at the wrong time.

IMPORTANT NOTE: All the words in *italics* in this script were written by Shakespeare.

Scene 1   An open place. Thunder and lightning.

Narrator: It was a cold wet day in Scotland in the year 1040. Three witches were waiting for Macbeth, a Scottish general, to pass by their heath (common).

Witch One: *When shall we three meet again?*
In thunder, lightning, or in rain?

Witch Two: *Where the place?*
Upon the heath

Witch Three: *There to meet with Macbeth*

Witch One: *Macbeth doth come.*

Narrator: And along came Macbeth, with his friend Banquo, fresh from winning a great battle.

Macbeth: *Speak if you can – what are you?*

Witch Three: *All hail, Macbeth, that shall be king hereafter.*

Narrator: The witches vanished. Banquo was shocked.

Banquo: I'm shocked. Did you hear her? *You shall be king!*

| Narrator: | Macbeth was overjoyed at the news. |
| Macbeth: | Wait till I tell my dear wife! |

Scene 2   Macbeth's castle

Macbeth: *My dearest love*
Duncan comes here tonight.
Narrator: Duncan was the old king.
Lady Macbeth: *And when goes hence?*
Macbeth: *Tomorrow, as he purposes.*
Lady Macbeth: He'll leave feet first,
inside a wooden box.
Make sharp your knife.
Leave all the rest to me.

Narrator: Her plan was to stab Duncan and leave the bloodstained knives on the sleeping guards. But Lady Macbeth didn't have the nerve to do it herself. She sent her husband.

Macbeth: *I have done the deed!*

Narrator: And so Macbeth became the Scottish king, just as the witches told him that he would. But he was worried that he'd be found out. His best friend knew about the witches – so the faithful, foolish Banquo had to die. Could Macbeth really kill his best old friend? Oh, no. He got someone else to do it.

Scene 3   A quiet corner of Macbeth's castle

Macbeth: *You know Banquo was your enemy*
Murderer: *True, my lord*
Macbeth: *So is he mine.*
Murderer: *We shall, my Lord, perform what you command us.*
Macbeth: Kill him! It must be done tonight.

Narrator: So Macbeth had his best friend Banquo killed. But then his ghost came back to haunt Macbeth. As he sat down to dine, the blood-soaked shape appeared . . .

Macbeth:	*Never shake thy gory locks at me!*
	Quit my sight! Let the earth hide thee!
	Thy bones are marrowless, thy blood cold.
	Hence, horrible shadow!
Narrator:	Lady Macbeth sent the guests home.
Lady Macbeth:	*A kind good night to all!*

Narrator: But by now the lords of Scotland knew the truth – Macbeth had killed their old king, Duncan, and the rest. Lord Macduff went off to England to get help. So Macbeth took it out on Macduff's family and had them murdered too.

Meanwhile, Lady Macbeth was going mad, imagining her hands were stained with blood . . .

Scene 4   Macbeth's castle

Lady Macbeth:	*Yet here's a spot.*
	Out, damned spot!
	Out, I say!
	Yet who would have
	thought the old man
	had so much blood in him?

Narrator: And so she killed herself. Macbeth was left alone. When Macduff heard about his family's death he came back home to Scotland for revenge!

Macduff:	*Tyrant, show thy face!*
Macbeth:	*Of all men else I have avoided thee,*
	My soul is too much charged with blood of thine.
Macduff:	*I have no words;*
	My voice is in my sword
Narrator:	They fight and Macduff kills Macbeth.
Macbeth:	That's life.
Narrator:	The end!

Shakespeare was careful to show that the rightful ruler, Malcolm, won in the end. The message to the audience was: "Don't try to overthrow your king. You will only end up dead." As Macbeth did in the play, or as Catesby and Guy Fawkes did in real life.

On the other hand, another playwright, Ben Jonson, wrote *Eastward Hoe*, a play which showed the court of King James as a lot of silly people with squeaky Scottish accents. Jonson ended up in prison! Some historians believe Ben Jonson was released because he promised to spy on the Catholics and he may have helped to uncover the Gunpowder Plot.

The Happy Hunter

Visitors to the theatre loved to see cruelty and death on stage, but these were cruel times in which to live. One of the cruellest of men was King James himself.

Many noble men and women enjoyed hunting, but James was obsessed with it. He preferred killing animals to ruling the country and often neglected his royal duties to go off hunting.

In Henry VIII's day it was usual for hundreds of deer to be rounded up then released in time for the king's hunting party to watch the hounds massacre them. The ladies gathered round to wash their hands in the blood – they believed it would keep their skin white.

James was just as vicious. He rode wildly behind the hounds. As soon as a dog pulled down a deer then James jumped off his horse and cut the throat of the animal. He would often playfully splash his hunting friends with the blood. He would catch far more deer than he or his court could possibly eat.

He hunted hares and used his hawks to catch larks. He enjoyed watching cock-fights and loved watching bears or bulls being baited to death. He even had a special pit of his own built for bear-baiting.

Once a bear was to be executed for killing a child. James brought it to his pit and set one of his lions to fight and destroy it. Unfortunately for James his lion refused to fight the bear!

This was the man who found the Gunpowder Plotters in his power. Would he be the sort of man to spare their lives . . . or at least spare them the terrible death of hanging, drawing and quartering? What do you think?

4. THE EVENTS FILE

Killing the King

Everyone remembers the fifth of November – even 400 years after the event. Why? It's not as if James's escape from death was a rare event.

Killing King James was a sort of hobby with people! The only surprise is that no one ever actually succeeded. These are some of the plots against the king . . .

1595 The Wizard Earl's attacks

The plotters: Francis Bothwell, known as 'The Wizard Earl' had tried to destroy James through witchcraft with the help of Agnes Sampson and a group of witches. When magic failed he decided to use force.

The plan: In the early 1590s Bothwell wanted to capture and imprison James. The earl had a band of soldiers to help him. James could not afford an army or even a proper bodyguard. The earl simply had to pick the right moment, walk into James's palace and take him.

What happened: On 27 December 1591 Bothwell marched into Holyrood Palace in Edinburgh where James was living at the time. James fled to a tower and locked Bothwell out. Bothwell's gang of ruffians set fire to the door and tried to break it down with hammers. A group of people from the town rushed to James's aid and drove off Bothwell . . . for a time. James offered a reward to anyone who would kill Bothwell. He avoided capture for two years and returned to attack James at the Falkland Palace. Again the strength of the palace defences defeated Bothwell. The next year he was back at Holyrood. James came face to face with Bothwell, kneeling with his sword. James rushed to the queen's bedroom crying, "Treason!" – but the bedroom door was locked. James was

The Bye Plot (or the 'Surprise' Treason)

The plotters: Catholics who felt that James was going to persecute them. The leaders were two priests, William Watson and William Clarke.

The plan: The plotters planned to kidnap James on Midsummer night 1603. Once he was their prisoner they would make him change the laws of the country to give Catholics freedom to worship as they wanted.

What happened: Government spies knew all about the plot very quickly. Watson and Clarke travelled round the country asking Catholic lords to support the kidnap of the king. Some agreed – some simply betrayed the plotters to the king's ministers. Clarke, Watson and some Catholic lords were arrested and tried.

What happened to the plotters? Clarke and Watson were found guilty. They were executed and, from one report, "very bloodily handled". The head of the Catholic Church, Pope Clement VIII, said they were nothing to do with him and deserved their deaths. King James offered to pardon any other Catholics who confessed.

The Main Plot

The plotters: Sir Walter Ralegh (who was angry because he lost his post as Captain of the Guard) and the Earl of Northumberland.

The plan: To kill King James and place his cousin, Lady Arabella Stuart, on the English and Scottish thrones.

What happened: When the Bye Plot was uncovered, a man called George Brooke was arrested. He not only betrayed the Bye plotters but talked about Ralegh and the Main Plot too. Ralegh was arrested and locked in the Tower of London where he made a feeble attempt to kill himself and failed.

What happened to the plotters? Brooke was executed even though he'd given the king all the help he needed to uncover the plot. The other plotters were taken to the scaffold to be executed, they said their last goodbyes . . . then were told that the king had spared them. (This seems to have been King James's cruel little joke.) King James had Ralegh locked in prison – so he could take his land and wealth – and finally released him in 1617. Ralegh was allowed to lead an expedition to the Orinoco River in South America in a search for gold. He fought against some Spanish ships and the furious Spanish insisted that he be executed. When Ralegh came home (without gold) James agreed to the execution – but the excuse James gave was the old Main Plot.

5. THE FAITH FILE

People in Tudor and Stuart times knew very little about science. So when something strange happened they said it was an 'act of God'. They believed God could do *anything*. They all agreed that there was a heaven for those who behaved themselves and hell for those who didn't. (King James believed that your trip to heaven or hell was decided at the moment you were born!)

The big problem was that the different types of Christian religion couldn't agree about how they should worship their God. Protestant rulers (like Elizabeth I and James I) passed laws to make everyone attend Protestant church services. If you didn't, then you had to pay a very heavy fine each month and often ended up in jail. The cost ruined some wealthy Catholic families – it even made some angry enough to wish James was dead.

This was the problem that caused so much trouble for the Tudor and Stuart monarchs.

What would you have done if you had been a Catholic?

Roman Catholics (like the Gunpowder Plotters), who were known as Romanist Catholics until 1623, believed
† that God gave power to the Pope in Rome who gave it in turn to kings. (James I hated this idea.)
† Romanist Catholics worshipped God with prayers in Latin, in fine churches with paintings and statues of religious scenes.
† the Spanish were Romanist Catholics and were prepared to go to war with countries like England to make everyone a Romanist Catholic.

Protestants like King James believed

✟ that God gave power directly to a king or queen. (James liked this idea!)

✟ that worshipping images (paintings and statues) in churches was evil. They tried to destroy all images.

✟ that churches should be plain and services simple. James arranged to have the Bible printed in English instead of Latin so everyone who could read could understand it.

Puritans believed

✟ that God was accessible to every human being, so you didn't need bishops in fine robes to tell you what to do.

✟ that they should obey the king – but they refused to believe that his power came directly from God. (James *hated* this idea. His son, Charles I, hated it even more. This was the argument that eventually led to Charles having his head cut off in 1649.)

✟ that worshipping images in churches was evil and they also hated religious celebrations. When they took over in 1649 they banned Christmas!

Did you know?
James opened his second Parliament in April 1614 with Puritans and the bishops they hated in the same procession. When a bishop fell off his horse a Puritan laughed . . . he laughed so much that he fell off his horse and broke his arm!

The Castle Killers

Lancaster in Tudor and Stuart times was the chief town in Lancashire . . . and Lancashire was England's most Catholic county. Lancaster Castle probably saw more Catholics punished than any other city except London and its castle was as deadly as the Tower of London itself. The executions John or Ellie could have seen included . . .

1597 Edmund Hartley executed
      Crime: murder by witchcraft
1600 Edward Thwing and Robert Nutter executed
      Crime: being Catholic priests
1601 Thurstan Hunt and Robert Middleton executed
      Crime: being Catholic priests
1604 Lawrence Bailey hanged
      Crime: rescuing a Catholic priest

All these executions would have been carried out in public as an example to the local people.

In the story, John's father, welcomed the chance to dispose of Catholics. But by 1628 a witness' report showed things had changed. Two Catholics were due to be executed but, according to the report:

No man could be persuaded to carry out the execution except a butcher. But he was so ashamed to do the job himself he paid a servant five pounds to do it for him. The servant, however, took the money then ran away. He was replaced as executioner by a deserter from the army who came to be detested by the good people of Lancaster.

Many people who attended the executions did not come for a bit of gruesome entertainment, the way they did in London. There were many Catholics there who came in tribute to the priests who were dying for their religion. They came to pray, not to gloat.

The priests became heroes, not villains. James didn't understand this too well. The Gunpowder Plotters were meant to be villains. To some they remain heroes too.

The Superstitious Stuarts

People in Stuart times were very superstitious. They believed in God . . . but they also believed in ghosts and the supernatural as these stories of the time show . . .

The cursed king

James was fascinated by witchcraft and the devil. He probably learned about witchcraft when he went to Denmark to meet his new bride, Anne. On his return to Scotland in 1590 he heard there were witches in North Berwick who were plotting to kill him . . . through a witchcraft curse! It was claimed that they threw a mixture of cats and joints of dead bodies into the North Sea as he was sailing across it. This raised a storm which almost wrecked James's ship.

James survived, heard of the plot and sent for the witches. He questioned their leader, Agnes Sampson. To his amazement the woman repeated to James some of the things he had whispered to his wife on the night of his wedding – words that no one but James and Anne could have heard.

James was so absorbed by the subject of witchcraft that he wrote a book about it in 1597 called *Demonology*. There is no proof that he ever saw any Lancaster witches (as in the story) but it is quite possible.

BUT . . . if Agnes Sampson and her friends were *really* plotting with the devil, how come the storm failed to sink James's ship? Is the devil so feeble that he can't wreck a small wooden ship?

–76–

The Spooky Stuarts

The phantom face

By February 1606 the Gunpowder Plotters were dead. Catesby had been shot, Guy Fawkes executed and all his powder safely buried. There was just the small matter of the Catholic priests to deal with. After all, the people of England had to be shown that the real villain wasn't Guy Fawkes . . . it was the Pope and his Catholic Church!

So the Earl of Salisbury had some of the remaining plotters tortured until they admitted that a Catholic priest, Father Henry Garnet, was part of the plot and had encouraged them to murder James. Father Garnet was captured, tortured and brought to trial. He was found guilty, of course, and sentenced to be hanged, drawn and quartered.

There was a lot sympathy for Father Garnet. Secret Catholics believed he was a martyr – dying for his religion. The superstitious people of the time believed that any relic of Garnet's death would be very holy.

Mrs Griffiths from Drury Lane in London was one of these Catholics. Now she couldn't bring herself to watch the execution – all that blood and pain would upset her too much – but she persuaded young John Williamson to bring something back from the scene. Anything.

John moved close to the platform where Father Garnet was being butchered. The platform was covered in straw – that would make mopping up easier. He snatched one piece of straw that still had an ear of corn on it. It was splashed with a drop of Father Garnet's precious blood. He took it to Mrs Griffiths, who put her hero's blood-drop in a box, put it away, and forgot about it for six weeks.

When she next looked at it she saw an incredible sight. The blood had formed itself into a pattern, a human face. She knew at once it was the face of the executed priest! His eyes were closed, his beard spotted with blood and there was a red ring round his neck where his head had been cut off.

The Catholics took great heart. The ear of corn was a miracle. It showed that Garnet was a saint and had died an innocent hero.

BUT . . . King James's government ordered an inquiry into this 'miracle'. By then the straw had vanished. One man who had seen the miraculous face said it could have been drawn with a fine pencil. A painter said it would have been easy to fake. The government report said the whole thing was a fraud . . . but, then, they *would* say that, wouldn't they?

The petrified plotters

On 2 February 1605 the Gunpowder Plotters had tunnelled from their house to the walls of the Houses of Parliament. That's when their problems really began. Those walls were about 4 metres thick. For two months they struggled to break through the stone until something strange and terrifying happened.

From deep within the wall the diggers heard the booming ring of some huge bell. They stopped work and called for Guy Fawkes to come down from guarding the house and listen. Fawkes was the expert. They hoped he could explain this mystery. Guy Fawkes listened while the bell kept tolling but was as puzzled and frightened as the others. It sounded like a funeral bell and a terrible warning. The men decided that evil spirits were to blame. They went to a friendly Catholic priest who gave them holy water. When they sprinkled this on the wall the ringing stopped.

They began work again but a minute later the bell began ringing again. Only the holy water could stop it and only for a little while. This went on for several days until suddenly the ringing stopped and never returned.

Soon afterwards they heard the rushing sound that was coal being delivered to the cellar above. That was when they discovered they could rent the cellar and save all the digging. The tunnel was abandoned and the mystery of the bell was never solved.

BUT . . . this story was told by a priest, Father Oswald Greenaway, who was suspected of helping the plotters but escaped to the Continent. No one else told this story and the plotters were all dead so they could not confirm it. Is it true? Or did Father Greenaway make it up? Why would he want to make up such a story? It's another mystery of history.

The Fawkes phantom

Guy Fawkes was questioned in a room in the King's House at the Tower. It had been built in Henry VIII's reign for the Tower's Governor to live in. King Henry's second wife, Anne Boleyn, spent the night in it before her execution.

For many years after the Gunpowder Plot soldiers swore that Guy Fawkes haunted that room.

BUT . . . the story started with a sentry who saw Guy Fawkes' ghost late one night. Did he see Guy's ghost? Or in the flickering light of a guttering candle did he just imagine it? The sentry admitted he was drunk at the time. So it's not too much of a mystery!

The thirteenth man

Thirteen was considered an unlucky number then, just as it is today. Some people say this superstition comes from the account in the Bible of the Last Supper. Jesus sat down to supper with his twelve disciples making thirteen at the table – the next day he was betrayed by Judas.

There were just five plotters who began the tunnel under Parliament. They were lucky to discover a cellar in a perfect place to lay their powder. But as 5 November grew closer they brought in more people to help. The last man, Francis Tresham, was the thirteenth. No sooner had Tresham joined than things started to go wrong. The warning letter ended up in the Earl of Salisbury's hands, Guy Fawkes was caught and the plotters were captured or killed.

Some historians believe Tresham was 'planted' by the Earl of Salisbury and betrayed the plotters. Tresham was taken to the Tower for questioning and he died there. Three doctors certified that he died of an illness. Some suspicious historians believe that he died under torture. But one historian has a fantastic theory about the thirteenth man. He believes Tresham escaped!

The idea is that Tresham had done such a good job for Salisbury that the chief minister arranged his escape. A woman came to visit Tresham and brought female clothes – the guards were changed and two women walked out . . . one of them Tresham in disguise. Very unlikely, but if it's true then he was lucky thirteen!

Guy Fawkes was born on 13 April.

BUT . . . although, thirteen was unlucky for the plotters James was superstitious about the number five. The Gowrie Plot in Scotland had taken place on a Tuesday the fifth of the month. The Gunpowder Plot took place on the fifth . . . and again it was a Tuesday! James said this proved, "It is the same devil that torments me, and it is the same God that rescues me."

6. THE WITCHCRAFT FILE

For hundreds of years before James came to the throne people had lived with witches. They went to the local witch for all sorts of help with their problems and were glad to have them in their community.

The Church didn't like magic . . . but the Elizabethan people still wanted to believe in it! Nearly every village had its own 'wise woman' or 'cunning man' or 'sorcerer' or 'witch'.

Elizabethans believed a witch or cunning man could cast spells to . . .

☦ find out who had stolen something.

☦ get rid of rats – the Pied Piper of Hamelin was a type of cunning man.

☦ cure toothache – and some of their herb mixtures probably helped.

☦ bring good luck to you – and we still believe in lucky charms like a horseshoe today.

☦ bring bad luck to your enemy – a curse to make them ill, unlucky or even die.

☦ protect your cattle from lightning – the family cow was a valuable possession for a poor family.

☦ make someone fall in love with you – very popular, this one.

☦ help you discover where treasure is buried – but this almost always failed!

☦ tell your fortune – no better or worse than horoscopes in today's newspapers.

☦ forecast the weather – not as scientific as today but their own methods must have been right some of the time.

What sort of spells did they use to produce this magic?

✝ to cure madness . . . release a live bat in the room of the sufferer.

✝ to find a criminal . . . write the names of suspects on pieces of paper and place them one at a time inside a Bible. The Bible will shake when the name of the criminal is put into it.

✝ to cure a mad dog . . . . feed it paper with a charm written on it.

✝ to cure a headache . . . boil some of the sufferer's hair in their urine then throw it on a fire.

✝ to cure animal sickness . . . tie herbs to the animal's tail or tap them with a magic wand.

✝ to cure heartache . . . cross garters over a patient's ears and mutter a spell.

✝ to cure aching bones jump in a river!

None of these magical tricks really work, of course. Sometimes the patient got better and the villagers said the witch had worked magic. Sometimes they got worse and the villagers said it was God's will. But no one really blamed or punished the cunning men or wise women for their mumbo-jumbo unless they were suspected of plotting against a king.

Of course if the local people turned against you then being a 'witch' could be fatal. If you were found guilty of using witchcraft to harm someone, then you'd be put in a pillory before being thrown into jail for a year. If you did it again you went to prison for life and lost all you owned. When James I came to the throne after Elizabeth then that second offence cost you your life.

Then there was always the chance your neighbours would simply decide you were a witch and attack you. The best way to draw the power from a witch, they believed, was to let the witch's blood out. A lucky witch would get away with a scratch on the face. Agnes Fenn was not lucky. In 1604, she was beaten and stabbed in the face – she was ninety-four years old. That's how afraid the people were of the devil's power.

They said you could recognise witches because . . .

✝ they had a habit of throwing back their hair.

✝ they never cried.

✝ they had tame 'devils' in the shape of pet toads or cats.

✝ they had a habit of twisting their fingers together.

James had a horror of witches and in 1604, the year when the Gunpowder Plotters first met, he passed a law that sentenced a witch to death for . . .

✝ making an agreement with an evil spirit.

✝ harming a living human or injuring cattle.

✝ using a dead body for a magic spell.

✝ mixing a love potion.

The Samwell Saga

In 1593, while James was interviewing witches in Scotland, there was the classic witchcraft trial of Mother Samwell in England.

Old Mother Samwell was a servant in Robert Throckmorton's house in Huntingdon. Suddenly strange things began to happen in the house. One of the children had a screaming fit while trying to pray . . .

The worst of the witch hunts began forty years after the Gunpowder Plot.

The Pendle Witches

Ellie in the story was accused of witchcraft and sentenced in Lancaster. The worst of the horrifying Lancaster witch trials happened five or six years later than this story. The 'witches' of that area had been active for fifty years before that, however. Young girls like Ellie were accused, tortured, found guilty and hanged.

What do you think?

Look at some facts and answer the questions "Yes" or "No".

The case against the Pendle 'witches' was built up by one rich and powerful man – Roger Nowell.

1.   Mother Demdike's granddaughter, Alizon, had seen Bessie Whittle commit robbery and reported her. Bessie would forgive the Demdike family, wouldn't she? *Yes/No?*

2.   Bessie accused Mother Demdike and her family of witchcraft. Bessie was a convicted thief. Can her honesty be trusted? *Yes/No?*

3.   Alizon had never been to court before. The magistrate began questioning her about Bessie Whittle's witchcraft accusations. As a witness Alizon would stay calm and tell the whole truth, wouldn't she. *Yes/No?*

4.   Alizon admitted that Mother Demdike had advised her (Alizon) to become a witch too. Alizon had seen her grandmother charm a can of milk so that a quarter-pound of

butter appeared in it. You believe such things are possible, don't you? *Yes/No?*

5.   Local farmer John Nutter asked Mother Demdike to cure a cow. Bessie said that Mother Demdike cursed the cow and it died. John Nutter *never* accused the old woman of cursing it. If

Nutter believed Mother Demdike was a witch then would he invite her to treat his cow? *Yes/No?*

6. John Nutter's father, Christopher, was ill for a few months before he died. He said he'd been cursed. He never said who cursed him. But he knew the Demdike

family, so it must have been them, mustn't it? *Yes/No?*

7. Alizon's brother, James, admitted he was a witch too. He said he'd quarrelled with a Mrs Townley at Easter 1610. He made a clay image of Mrs Townley, dried and crumbled it. As the clay crumbled Mrs Townley died. The records prove that Mrs Townley died on 25 October 1611 – eighteen months after James says he killed her. Never mind, he could still be guilty, couldn't he? *Yes/No?*

8. Alizon's nine-year-old sister Jennet was charged with killing Thomas Lister by witchcraft. When she was brought to Thomas Lister's corpse then "it bled fresh blood when she touched it". This is quite possible and it proves she was guilty. *Yes/No?*

9. The accused people were extremely poor. Mother Demdike had only one garment to wear. She was eighty years old and completely blind. Would the Devil treat his servants so badly? *Yes/No?*

10. They were not very popular because they were known to be lazy and ignorant, forever begging and stealing. Does this make them witches? *Yes/No?*

If you have ten *yes* answers then you'd make a really ruthless witch-finder!

Amazingly Roger Nowell must have said 'yes' to all of these questions. He had the whole family executed, although blind Mother Demdike died in the filthy, airless cell of Lancaster Castle's Well Tower Dungeon.

Did you know . . . ?

1. Prisoners could pay the jailer for the comfort of fresh straw – Mother Demdike and her family were too poor.

2. Prisoners could have extra, better food brought in by friends – Mother Demdike and her family had no friends.

3. The Pendle witches were spared the torture that Guy Fawkes and the Scottish witches suffered. It was against the law of England to torture witch suspects. But the conditions in the Well Tower dungeon were bad enough to make anyone suffer terribly.

4. Even then, not everyone believed in witchcraft. In 1584 Reginald Scot published a book which said there was no such thing. King James disagreed . . . and ordered that the book should be burned!

5. One of the chief Pendle witnesses was a girl called Jennet Device. She was just nine years old. Normally such a young child would not be able to give the evidence that sent her own mother, brother and sister to the gallows. But James I had argued in his book, *Demonology*, that witch trials were different – children could be heard in court. So James helped cause the deaths of these people.

6. James said you could even believe witchcraft stories told by madwomen and criminals.

7. Young Jennet's entire family was executed on Lancaster Moor, just outside the city. But that wasn't the end of witchcraft in her life. Twenty years later she was arrested on a charge of murder by witchcraft and ended up in Lancaster Castle's dungeons herself. Some of her fellow-prisoners were sent to London for questioning. James was dead by then, of course, and after three miserable years they were all finally set free. Lucky Jennet.

8. Lancashire was full of Catholic enemies of James –
the Gunpowder Plotters were on their way to
Lancashire when they were caught. A Protestant priest
said, "The vilest witches and sorcerers on earth are
Catholic priests." It suited James to link the Catholics
and witches and plots against the crown together.
As the Bible said, "Rebellion is a sin of witchcraft."
It also said, "You should not allow a witch to live."
Plotters, witches, Catholics – they were all the same
thing to James . . . and they all had to die.
9. King James liked witches to be burned, as they were
in Scotland. In England, however, the law said
they should be hanged and James never managed
to change this.
10 It wasn't until 1735 that James's laws on witchcraft
were abolished. By then hundreds had died in England
and Scotland. This was the power a king had who
believed in the devil. Laws against Catholics were still
in force a hundred years later. This was the power of
a Gunpowder Plot that made all Catholics seem as
dangerous as the man they called 'The Devil
in the vault' : Guy Fawkes.

Part Three
The truth about Guy Fawkes

12 November 1605

After my father had given me last-minute instructions I left the Tower and its grim secrets behind. Ellie's wrists were tied and I held the rope. Her head hung on her chest and she swayed in the saddle.

We rode along the north bank of the Thames and the bitter wind was in our faces. At least Sir William Waad had made sure we had good horses and warm riding cloaks. He also gave me a purse of money for expenses on the journey. He frowned as he said, "The Earl of Salisbury insisted on your having fifty pounds. God knows why," he shrugged and handed over the heavy leather purse. "Good luck," he said before he turned and walked stiffly back to his office. He didn't see that Ellie turned back and hurried to say goodbye to her lion cubs.

"They're the only thing I'll miss about this dreadful place," she'd sighed. "They're just poor innocent prisoners."

The streets of London were damp and muddy so it was a relief to reach the more open countryside. I stopped at the top of Highgate Hill and looked back at the walls of the city. The road to the left swung away to Lancaster and the north-west. I pulled out my knife. Ellie looked up blankly.

"You are going to stab me?" she asked. "Thank you. It's better than hanging."

I pulled her towards me and sliced through the rope on her wrists. She stared at me for a long time and slowly, slowly her face lit with a smile. "Why, John?"

"Because the earl told me to make sure justice was done. You are innocent . . . so justice demands that I set you free."

"They'll punish you, John. For letting a prisoner escape," she said.

"Perhaps."

"They will. You know it."

"Don't worry about me."

"Why shouldn't I? You've worried about me."

That was true. "Come with me, John," she said and the wind whipped at her words.

"Where to?"

"Somewhere in the east. Anywhere but Lancaster. You've nothing to go back there for, have you?"

I shook my head. "I have some money that the earl gave me," I said, cheering up. "I think we can make it!"

I slapped my horse into a canter and led the way down the road to the east. We didn't stop till near darkness when we found an inn with a glowing fire and good food. London, the Tower and its poor prisoners were fifty miles behind us, but I couldn't help thinking about them. "Who betrayed him?" I asked Ellie as we stared into the dying embers.

"He was an honest man," the girl began.

"He was a murderer!" I exclaimed.

"Yes, yes," she said impatiently. "What I meant was . . . he would give his word honestly and keep it. The trouble was he believed everyone else would do the same."

I nodded: "But they didn't."

"So, Robert Catesby sent for him and explained that

the only way for Catholics to live in peace was to get rid of James and his chief ministers. Guy could see the sense in that. But he knew that Catholic lords would be killed in the explosion too. Catesby promised they would be warned," she explained.

"So Catesby sent the letter! The leader of the plot betrayed himself!" I cried. One or two heads turned towards us in the tavern and I lowered my voice.

Ellie shook her head. "I asked Guy if Catesby had sent the letter but he thought not. Catesby was too far away at the time. And no other Catholic lords got warnings," she said.

"Catesby promised he would warn them," I said, puzzling over it.

She nodded her dark head slowly. "Catesby lied."

I thought about this for a while. "What else did he lie about?" I wondered.

"That's what Guy was wondering," Ellie said. "The officers knew exactly where to go to arrest him. He suffered two days of torture. He refused to name any of the other plotters – yet Waad knew the names already. He knew all about Catesby and the others. He only wanted Guy's confession so they would have the statement to read out in court."

"The Earl of Salisbury and the government knew all about the plot then. It would never have worked," I reckoned. "When did they find out."

Ellie frowned. "Maybe they always knew. Maybe the Earl of Salisbury set it up! Catesby was part of a rebellion against Elizabeth four years ago. The Earl of Salisbury spared Catesby's life . . ."

"And in return Catesby organised the Powder Plot?" I gasped. "Incredible. Maybe the earl wants something from us in return for sparing your life," I told her.

She gave a soft smile. "I don't think I could be of much

use to a man like the earl. But that's the way he works."

I thought about the clever little minister and the way his cunning mind worked. It was just possible. I tried to imagine what would happen next. "Surely he can't let Catesby go a second time," I argued.

Ellie looked back at the fire. "He doesn't have to. One of the things Waad said before Fawkes confessed. He said Catesby is dead. He died fighting to get away."

"That's handy for the Earl of Salisbury," I muttered. Then I brightened. "It's the first time Guy has been caught in a plot. He's told Waad all he knows. Maybe they'll let him go this time. Remember the way they let Catesby go last time!"

"I hope so," Ellie said and shuddered. "Otherwise they'll hang him, cut him open and behead him. It's a horrible way to die for such a brave man. And I wouldn't like to think of his head on London Bridge alongside all those other traitors."

"It's not as if he was a real plotter, is it? He was just a sort of tool in the Earl of Salisbury's plot, wasn't he?" I asked.

Ellie nodded. "Maybe Guy Fawkes will be spared," she agreed. "That's what happened after the last plot. They took the traitors on to the scaffold. Then, just before they executed them, they announced that the king had pardoned them. Maybe that will happen to Guy."

"Maybe," I agreed.

"Maybe," Ellie whispered. "I hope."

***

The Powder Plot was the talk of every tavern we stopped in on the way north. We reached York just before Christmas. We stayed there when the weather turned too cold and too wild to travel. I found a job helping a blacksmith while Ellie took a job helping in the kitchens of a large house in the city.

We met most evenings in a tavern in the shadow of the cathedral. The people of York were less excited about the plot than they had been in the south. "The Earl of Salisbury is a rich man," someone said to the blacksmith one day. "But a lot of his lands came from the Catholic Church when Henry VIII abolished it. If the Catholics get back in power then the Earl of Salisbury will lose a fortune. That's the real reason he hates the Catholics. It's not because he's a good little Protestant – it's not even because he loves that Scottish fool James! It's simple greed."

For speaking words of treason like that the man would have been in the Tower and under Waad's torturers in two minutes. Here, in York, people were freer with their opinions. We soon discovered it was because the city was Guy's birthplace. His family still lived there. No one could believe the son of York was the devil that the Earl of Salisbury was painting him.

News of the trial was slow in reaching us. It happened on 27 January 1606, almost three months after the arrest. The plotters were found guilty and sentenced to be hanged, drawn and quartered.

One thing still puzzled me. "Who wrote the letter?" I asked Ellie one evening.

She smiled – she smiled a lot these days – and said, "I've been wondering that too. I think the Earl of Salisbury wanted the plot to be uncovered in time but he couldn't suddenly announce that gunpowder had been found under Parliament. He needed to give the world some reason why he should search those cellars and catch Guy Fawkes."

"You mean the Earl of Salisbury sent the letter?" I asked.

Ellie shrugged. "I think he could have done. But he's too clever ever to be found out. We'll never really know."

"Then Guy Fawkes was betrayed by the Earl of Salisbury? The Earl can't let him be executed," I said.

"He must make sure Guy's pardoned."

"He should," Ellie agreed. "But he's a strange man." Ellie was so wise I sometimes wondered if she really did have witch powers. For that very night the news came that on 31 January Guy Fawkes was the last of the plotters to die at the bloodstained hands of the executioner.

There had been no pardon.

Within a month a thaw had come and the roads were clear enough to travel on. We'd used very little of the money the Earl of Salisbury had given us. "We can go now," I told Ellie one day.

"I've run far enough now," Ellie announced. "I'm staying here. You go if you want to."

The idea of going anywhere without her seemed unthinkable now. The idea that she should ever have been executed by my father was beyond belief. It was the Earl of Salisbury's plot that Ellie and I should end up looking after one another.

"I'm staying," I said. "With you."

She smiled. The Earl of Salisbury's plots usually worked.

EPILOGUE

Ellie, John and his father in the story are invented characters. The rest are true and most of the facts surrounding Guy Fawkes's arrest and imprisonment are true – though some of the documents we have from that time may have been forged or altered by the Earl of Salisbury's assistants.

In 1605 someone wrote to a friend in England:

I heard that some lords were in Parliament and a barrel of gunpowder was lit under them. It went off and most of them were blown up. I cannot believe so strange and desperate an act.

You can see that even in 1605 people didn't know quite what was going on! The story of the Gunpowder Plot had been twisted and changed hopelessly within a few weeks of its happening. We have very little chance of discovering the truth after almost 400 years.

This story has suggested that:

_ The earl of Salisbury knew of the plot at a very early stage.

_ He let it carry on till the last moment to see how many Catholics he could trap.

Many historians believe that is the truth. Other historians go further. They say :

_ The Earl of Salisbury set up the whole plot himself with Catesby's help.

_ Salisbury wrote the letter that betrayed them.

_ The gunpowder barrels were filled with harmless soil.

_ Guy Fawkes knew all about Salisbury's part in the plot.

_ Guy Fawkes let himself be caught and wrote a confession without ever being tortured.

_ He expected to be set free at the last minute. (In which case Guy must have had a real shock when he realised he was in fact going to die!)

On the other hand some historians still argue that:

_ The Earl of Salisbury knew nothing about the plot.

_ King James was saved by that last–minute search of Parliament.

We'll never be able to prove any of these ideas. You just have to look at the evidence and decide which is the most likely? What do you think?

It's a true mystery of history.